PLANET DOONESBURY

A DOONESBURY BOOK

PLANET DOONESBURY

BY G. B. TRUDEAU

Andrews McMeel
Publishing

Kansas City

"Vietnam is not a war anymore, it's a country."

—Saigon entrepreneur David Case

HEY, BABE, YOU GOT A PEN PAL IN VIETNAM?

SURE DO— GEORGE GILCREST!

WHO'S HE?

AN OLD ARMY BUDDY OF MINE. WE WERE IN THE 11TH ARMORED CAV TOGETHER...

WAIT A MINUTE! YOU WERE IN THE 11TH ARMORED CAVALRY REGIMENT?

YEAH. WHY?

I'M 99% SURE THAT WAS ELVIS' OUTFIT!

WOULDN'T BE SURPRISED— WE ROCKED!

THIS GEORGE WAS A GOOD FRIEND OF YOURS?

THE BEST!

WE WERE BUDS AT FIRE-BASE BUNDY IN THE DELTA. THE GUY WAS A COMPLETE WILD MAN—ESPECIALLY DURING DOWNTIME...

WE USED TO GO TO SAIGON AND... AND... UH...

AND WHAT?

RIDE THE MERRY-GO-ROUND. BACK-WARD. CRAZY STUNTS LIKE THAT.

SO WHAT'S YOUR FRIEND DOING IN VIETNAM?

WELL, HE'S INVOLVED IN SOME SORT OF JOINT VENTURE...

APPARENTLY YOU CAN'T REALLY DO BUSINESS THERE UNLESS YOU HAVE A VIETNAMESE PARTNER...

BASICALLY THE ARRANGEMENT IS YOU POUR IN A LOT OF MONEY, AND YOUR PARTNER SECURES ALL THE NECESSARY PERMITS.

PERMITS TO DO WHAT?

TO POUR IN MORE MONEY. IT SORT OF REMINDS ME OF THE WAR...

GEORGE THINKS VIETNAM IS THE NEXT ASIAN ECONOMIC POWERHOUSE, THAT WITH HER RESOURCES, THE SKY'S THE LIMIT!

HE FEELS THAT HE'S GOTTEN IN ON THE GROUND FLOOR, THAT RIGHT NOW IS A TIME OF EXTRAORDINARY INVESTMENT OPPORTUNITY!

YEAH, BUT IS HE ACTUALLY MAKING MONEY?

HE SAYS HE WILL BE. MAYBE. IT'S TOO SOON TO TELL, REALLY.

VIETNAM SOUNDS A LOT LIKE THE WEB.

WELL, HE'S ONLY ON HIS THIRD ROUND OF BRIBES.

SO WHAT ELSE DOES GEORGE SAY?

WELL, HE'S INVITING ME TO VISIT HIM IN VIETNAM...

MY GOSH... WOULD YOU EVEN CONSIDER IT?

WELL, I DON'T KNOW. MAYBE IT'S FINALLY TIME. IT MIGHT HELP EXORCISE A FEW DEMONS.

WHAT DO YOU MEAN?

WELL, LIKE MY NIGHTMARES. FOR YEARS, I'VE HAD THIS RECURRING DREAM ABOUT BEING TRAPPED IN A FIREFIGHT.

A FIREFIGHT? HERE IN L.A.?

YEAH. SO A CHANGE OF SCENERY MIGHT DO ME GOOD.

MAYBE I SHOULD GO BACK TO VIETNAM, BOOPSIE. AS A KIND OF CLOSURE.

BUT DON'T YOU HAVE LOTS OF BAD ASSOCIATIONS WITH VIETNAM?

WELL, SURE, OF COURSE. BUT ON ANOTHER LEVEL, I LOVED IT. IT'S THE DARK SECRET OF LOTS OF SOLDIERS— THEY LOVED COMBAT, ITS INTENSITY...

I DUNNO... IT'S HARD TO EXPLAIN.

YOU DON'T HAVE TO, B.D.— I UNDERSTAND.

NO, YOU DON'T, BOOPSIE— UNLESS YOU'VE...

B.D., I SERVED IN THE PUNIC WARS. SO DON'T PATRONIZE ME.

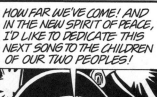

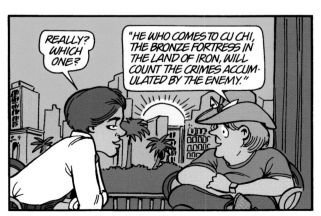

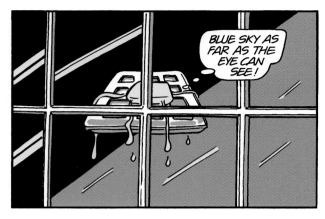

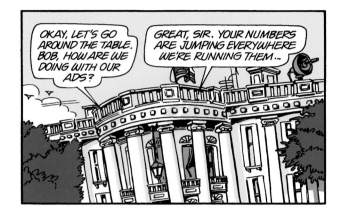

CAST KEY

Progenitor of BUTTS (26), ex-ad man **MIKE** (6), son of the **WIDOW D.** (15) and brother of Dr. Whoopie rep **SAL** (14), is freshly divorced from artist **J.J.** (16) (lover of **ZEKE** (17) and daughter of legal eagle **JOANIE** (1), who is married to reporter **RICK** (10)), and has moved with daughter **ALEX** (7) to Seattle, where he's fallen in love with GenX coder **KIM** (5) while working for technocrat **BERNIE** (34), a former roommate (at a college presided over by **KING** (28) and chaplained by **SCOT** (18)), as is state trooper **B.D.** (8) (friend of fellow vet **RAY** (19) and former adversary of **PHRED** (25)); his superstarlet wife **BOOPSIE** (9), who is repped by **SID** (29) and whose daughter **SAM** (2) is nannied by retired tannist **ZONKER** (4) (honorific nephew of **DUKE** (12), who with son **EARL** (11) has left love-slave **HONEY** (13) to settle in Las Vegas); and gay radio jock **MARK** (3) (son of financier **PHIL** (30), a friend of oil tycoon **JIM** (35)), who is a colleague of correspondent **ROLAND** (20), interviewer of homeless couple **ALICE** (24) and **ELMONT** (23), and a fan of **JIMMY** (22), whose benefit record for **GINNY** (32), wife to cookie czar **CLYDE** (31), failed to help her defeat **LACEY** (21) in her bid for Congress now led by **NEWT** (27) in opposition to **BILL** (33).

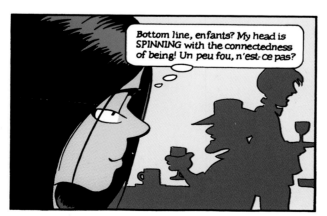

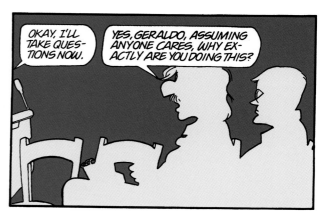

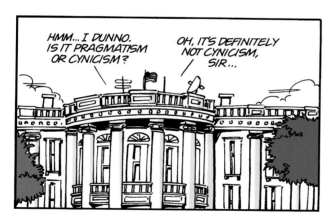

55

56

WELCOME BACK TO CONTINUING CONVENTION COVERAGE ON "ALL THINGS RECONSIDERED"...

WE'RE GOING TO GO NOW TO OUR MOST EXCELLENT FLOOR REPORTER, ELMONT DOE, STANDING BY ON THE CONVENTION FLOOR...

ELMONT? CAN YOU HEAR ME? TAKE IT AWAY, BUDDY!

THANKS, MARK. I'M STANDING HERE WITH GOVERNOR COLIN POWELL...

WHAT? WHERE?

AND AS THE DEMOCRATS CONTINUE ON THEIR LONG ELECTION-YEAR SLOG TOWARD THE RIGHT...

...THEY SEEM TO HAVE LOST THEIR SOUL, THEIR VERY IDENTITY AS CHAMPIONS OF SOCIETY'S DISPOSSESSED!

ARE THE DEMOCRATS STILL THE PARTY OF COMPASSION? OUR MAN ELMONT POLLS THE DELEGATES! ELMONT?

THANKS, MARK. GOVERNOR, CAN I HAVE A QUARTER?

YOU'LL HAVE TO WORK FOR IT. GET ME A BEER.

...AND WE FEEL CLINTON'S DEFENSE OF THE ANTI-GAY MARRIAGE BILL WAS A TERRIBLE SLAP IN THE FACE!

WELL, THERE YOU HAVE IT, MARK—ANOTHER DELEGATE ABANDONED, FORSAKEN BY HIS OWN PARTY!

THIS IS ONE GAY, DEMOCRATIC ACTIVIST WHO'S FEELING VERY LONELY JUST NOW, MARK!

UM...IS HE CUTE?

BEATS ME. I DON'T HAVE MY CONTACTS IN.

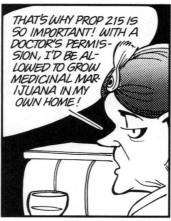

YEAH, WHAT'S GOING ON WITH THE PAULA JONES CASE?

WELL, THE SUPREME COURT WILL BE HEARING ORAL ARGUMENTS IN JANUARY...

ORAL ARGUMENTS? THAT SOUNDS SORT OF OBSCENE ALL BY ITSELF!

WHAT AN APPALLING COMMENT, YOUNG MAN!

IT IS PRECISELY THAT KIND OF UTTER DISRESPECT AND INCIVILITY THAT HAS MADE PUBLIC SERVICE SO INHOSPITABLE FOR PEOPLE WHO GENUINELY WANT TO MAKE A DIFFERENCE IN GOVERNMENT!

WHATEVER. SO DID CLINTON FLASH HER?

WHAT?

YOU DON'T HAVE TO TAKE THIS, JOANIE...

YOUNG MAN, I DON'T THINK THAT QUESTION...

SO WHAT'S THE DEAL ON CLINTON'S "DISTINGUISHING" MARKS?

OKAY, THAT'S QUITE ENOUGH, SON!

SCOT, I CAN HANDLE THIS...

LISTEN, I'VE KNOWN THIS GAL FOR OVER 20 YEARS! SHE'S A CLASS ACT! SHE DOESN'T DESERVE THIS VULGAR INQUISITION!

SCOT!

C'MON, JOANIE— I'LL DRIVE YOU HOME!

THAT HAS TO BE THE SINGULARLY MOST EMBARRASSING MOMENT OF MY LIFE...

WELL, I THOUGHT SO. THAT'S WHY I RESCUED YOU.

SCOT, THAT WAS WHAT WAS SO EMBARRASSING! I'M AN ASSISTANT TO THE ATTORNEY GENERAL OF THE UNITED STATES! I THINK I COULD HAVE HANDLED THE SITUATION BY MYSELF!

OH.

OH? JUST OH?

UM... WOULD YOU LIKE TO DRIVE?

MR. PRESIDENT, ABC NEWS HAS RECEIVED WORD THAT CHELSEA HAS APPLIED TO WALDEN COLLEGE. CAN YOU CONFIRM THAT?

WALDEN COLLEGE? HEE, HEE... RIGHT!

UM... SO SHE HASN'T?

DON'T BE ABSURD. WHAT DO YOU THINK MY DAUGHTER IS—AN IDIOT?

I CAN'T STAND IT...

WOW! HE SAID OUR NAME! ON NATIONAL TV!

WELL, THEN, WHO DO YOU THINK DID SEND IN THE APPLICATION, SWEETHEART?

I'LL BET IT WAS MAX!

MAX?

MAXWELL MERTZ, MY LAB PARTNER! HE'S ALWAYS TELLING ME I'M HEADED FOR A LOSER COLLEGE...

MAX IS OKAY, BUT HIS SENSE OF HUMOR IS TOTALLY LAME. GOD KNOWS WHAT HE PUT ON THE APPLICATION ESSAY...

"AND WHEN WE'RE JUST FAMILY, DAD LIKES TO EAT WITH HIS FEET."

SOME GREAT TIDBITS, EH, SIR?

OKAY, LISTEN UP, EVERYONE. THIS IS MAXWELL MERTZ FROM CHELSEA'S CLASS, AND HE HAS SOMETHING TO TELL YOU. MAX?

UM... YEAH, HERE'S THE DEAL ON THE APPLICATION. WE WERE JUST TRYING TO WEIRD OUT CHEL BY ENROLLING HER IN A JOKE COLLEGE, OKAY?

IT WAS LIKE, A TOTALLY IMMATURE THING TO DO, AND ON BEHALF OF THE ENTIRE SENIOR CLASS, I'D LIKE TO APOLOGIZE TO ANYONE WHOSE HEAD WE MESSED WITH.

AND ANOTHER SCANDAL COMES DRIBBLING OUT!

INCREDIBLE! WONDER IF I CAN WORK THIS INTO MY PAULA JONES PIECE...

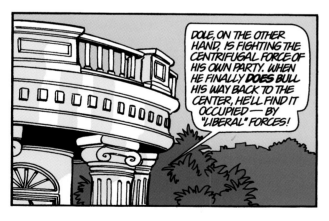

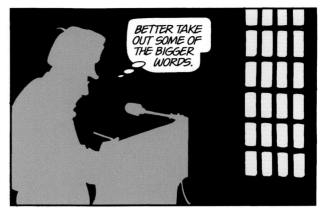

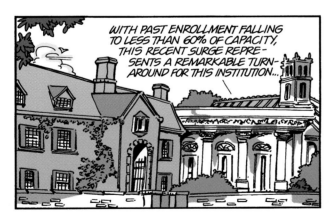

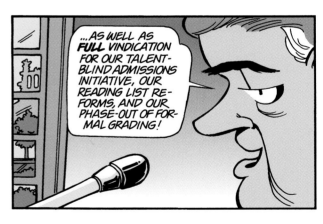

82

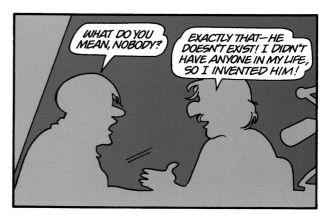

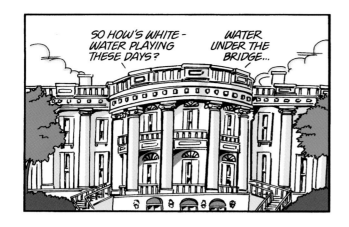

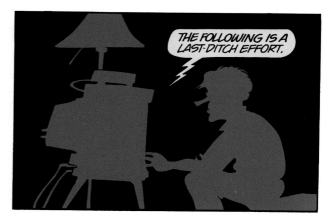

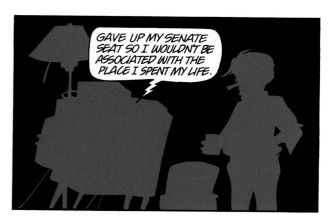

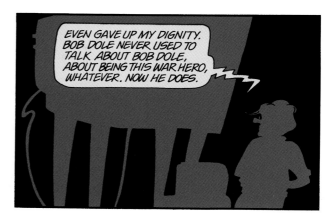

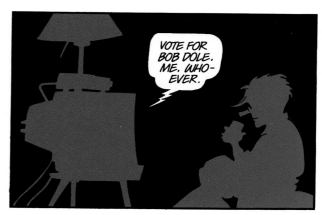

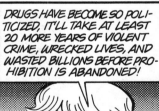

DAD-STER!

MOMMY JUST CALLED! SHE'S BEEN SELLING OUTDOOR SCULPTURES TO ALL THE BIG COMPUTER GUYS IN TOWN!

OH... WELL, THAT'S GREAT, BABE...

LIKE, FOR HOW MUCH?

KIM, J.J. WOULDN'T BE DIS- CUSSING MONEY WITH...

$400,000 A POP!

YOUR MOMMY'S MAKING **HOW** MUCH, ALEX?

$400,000 A SCULP- TURE...

NOT ONLY THAT, BUT SHE SAYS SHE HAS A **ZILLION** ORDERS!

WHY ON EARTH WOULD J.J. DISCUSS HER FINANCES WITH AN EIGHT-YEAR-OLD?

SHE SAID SHE WANTED ME TO SEND YOU A MESSAGE.

YOU MEAN, **GIVE** ME A MESSAGE.

NO, NO, SHE SPECIFICALLY SAID "SEND."

YOU KNOW, MIKE, SINCE SHE'S DOING SO WELL, MAYBE YOU **SHOULD** LET J.J. HELP WITH CHILD SUPPORT...

NO WAY! SHE'S ONLY TRYING TO REASSERT CONTROL!

I BARELY RECOGNIZE HER ANYMORE! J.J. USED TO BE SO GIVING, SO POSITIVE, SO SUP- PORTIVE OF ME AND MY DREAMS...

YOU CAN'T IMAGINE HOW SPE- CIAL SHE WAS! SHE LIT UP MY LIFE, JUST TRANSFORMED IT! I WISH I KNEW WHAT DROVE HER AWAY FROM ME...

MAYBE YOU USED TO DRONE ON ABOUT OTH- ER WOMEN.

NO... NO, I DON'T THINK THAT WAS IT...

HEY, FUTURE STEP-MOMSTER— STILL WORKING ON THE GUEST LIST?

UH-HUH. I'VE GOT IT DOWN TO UNDER 300.

300? YOU *KNOW* 300 PEOPLE?

YUP. NOW I'M ORGANIZING THEM IN CATEGORIES SO I CAN PRIORITIZE THEM.

CATEGORIES? WHAT SORT OF CATEGORIES?

OKAY, WELL, LIKE THIS COLUMN IS OLD BOYFRIENDS...

WOW! DADDY BEAT OUT *ALL* THOSE GUYS?

HOLD IT!

BOYFRIENDS? YOU WANT TO INVITE BOYFRIENDS?

FORMER BOYFRIENDS! THEY'RE MY BUDS NOW, MY TRIBE!

I UNDERSTAND, BUT THIS IS OUR *WEDDING*, KIM!

SO? I DON'T SEE WHAT THE BIG DEAL IS.

LOOK, I JUST THINK WE SHOULD HAVE SOME GROUND RULES FOR THE GUEST LIST, OKAY?

LIKE WHAT?

WELL, LIKE, NO PEOPLE WHO'VE SLEPT WITH THE BRIDE.

OH, GREAT! SO WE ONLY INVITE *YOUR* FRIENDS?

MICHAEL, I REALLY DON'T SEE WHY YOU'RE HAVING SUCH A PROBLEM WITH MY INVITING A FEW MALE FRIENDS TO THE WEDDING...

YOU DON'T?

NO. I MEAN, YOU'VE GOT ALL THESE WOMEN ON *YOUR* LIST...

LIKE WHO?

WELL, LIKE, WHO'S THIS JOANIE CAUCUS?

UM...MY FORMER MOTHER-IN-LAW.

OH! HOW *SPECIAL*! SHALL WE SEAT HER AT THE HEAD TABLE?

WHITEWATER INDY COUNSEL *KEN STARR* VISITS THE SITE OF HIS POSTPONED DREAMS.

OH, WOW— IT'S OUR DEAN-/ DESIGNATE!

WELCOME TO MALIBU LAW, MR. STARR!

THANKS, BOYS! ON A BREAK FROM CLASSES?

UH... YEAH, THERE'S A LOT OF PRESSURE ON US HERE. I HOPE YOU'LL BE ABLE TO DO SOMETHING ABOUT IT.

WHAT YEAR ARE YOU, SON?

UM... I DUNNO. FIFTH?

NO WAY, MAN. WE ENROLLED TOGETHER IN '88.

YOU'RE GOING TO *LOVE* IT HERE, DEAN-DESIGNATE! THE LAW SCHOOL IS *WAY* EXCELLENT!

WHAT ARE YOU STUDYING, YOUNG MAN?

WELL, SINCE O.J., I'VE BEEN LEANING TOWARD CRIMINAL LAW.

YOU WANT TO BE A PROSE-CUTOR? OR A PUBLIC DEFENDER?

NO, I WANT TO BE A SURFER. THAT'S REALLY WHY I CAME HERE — TO GET GOOD ENOUGH TO TURN PRO.

SERVING THE PUBLIC IS MY BACK-UP POSITION.

MINE, TOO.

HEY... IT'S *HIM!*

WHO?

KENNETH STARR— THE WHITEWATER PROSECUTOR AND FUTURE DEAN AT PEPPERDINE!

KENNETH WHO? WHAT'S WHITE-WATER? WHERE'S PEPPERDINE?

I'M GOING TO GET HIS AUTOGRAPH. YOU WANT ONE?

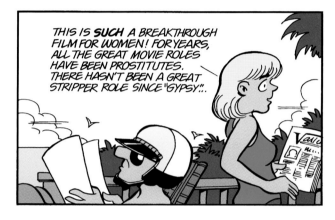

WONDER IF JEFF IS SPEAKING WITH US TODAY...

...OR IF THERE'S BEEN ANOTHER OVERNIGHT HORMONE SURGE.

HEY, RICK, WHATEVER HAPPENED WITH CHELSEA CLINTON'S APPLICATION TO WALDEN?

IT WAS WITHDRAWN. THE KID WHO SENT IT IN APOLOGIZED, AND NONE OF US WROTE ANOTHER WORD ABOUT IT.

YOU KNOW, IT'S KIND OF AMAZING HOW PROTECTIVE THE PRESS HAS BECOME OF HER...

I THINK BECAUSE CHELSEA'S SUCH A NICE, BRIGHT, POLITE, WELL-ADJUSTED TEEN-AGER, WE'VE ALL DECIDED SHE'S A NATIONAL TREASURE.

I MEAN, IT'S SO RARE THAT...

GOT IT, DAD! MESSAGE RECEIVED LOUD AND CLEAR, OKAY?

WAS THAT REALLY NECESSARY, RICK?

WHAT? WHAT JUST HAPPENED?

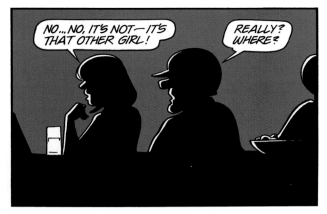

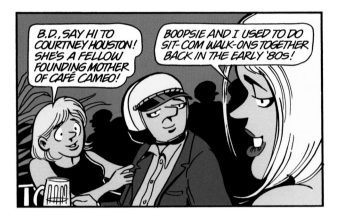

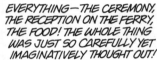